1. Slice the clay slightly thicker than the thickest setting on the pasta machine.

2. Flatten the clay slab with the acrylic brayer.
3. Fold the flattened slab piece and run it

through a pasta mach. on the thickest setting. Repeat until the clay is uniformly warm and soft.

Method One

This is the best method to use for 'new' clay that is fairly soft when you open the package. Remember to always 'condition' the clay as it will work better and the polymers will adhere together better.

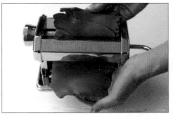

1. Cut the pieces the thickness of the thickest setting of the pasta machine.

2. Combine them together and run them through until the clay is uniformly warm and soft.

3. Run them through your pasta machine on the thickest setting.

Method Two

There will be more pieces to combine with this method.

How to Measure Polyclay

The color mix instructions will state blocks, sections or fractions of a section. To divide a block of clay, press the side of the Marxit indicated in the instructions onto the clay. Use the slicing blade to cut the clay where indicated.

How to Make a Skinner Blend

This method of creating sheets of clay that perfectly gradate from one color to another was introduced to the polymer clay community by artist Judith Skinner.

1. Select two colors of clay and roll each color through the thickest setting of the pasta machine. Lay one sheet atop the other and cut a right angle triangle shape. Separate the two triangles and press the diagonal sides of the triangles together as shown, offsetting the corners.

Cut and remove the corners to make a rectangle shape
2. Fold this sheet in half so that the same color edge lies on the same color edge.
3. On the thickest setting, place the fold on the rollers and roll through.

Repeat, folding and rolling until the sheet is blended from one color to the other and there are no streaks. The strip nearest the pasta machine was cut from a sheet that has been rolled through 10 times. The other strip shows what the blend looks like after it has been rolled through 25 times.

See Project on page 19

Inkjet Transfers and Acrylic Paint Effects

Donna Kato

Favorite Pendants

This is one of my favorite pendants, incorporating inkjet transfers and various acrylic paint techniques. After the components are made, they'll be set in Black polyclay.

Epson Glossy Photo paper, not premium paper, is required for flawless transfers. Because the transfers are translucent, they will be affected by the color of the clay on which they are made. For this reason, I suggest transferring onto light colored clay.

I hope you enjoy this technique!

Donna Kato

Combining faux brocade, faux leaf and faux silkscreen with rubber stamping and image transfer opens a new realm of possibilities for the clay artist. Feel free to immerse yourself in some playful experimentation with these techniques. The results are thrilling and incredibly beautiful.

Technique 1: Inkjet Transfer

Technique 1... MATERIALS: Kato (Liquid Polyclay Clear Medium; Polyclay: White, Translucent or Pearl) • Color inkjet image printed on *Epson* Glossy photo paper • Deli wrap • Sharp scissors

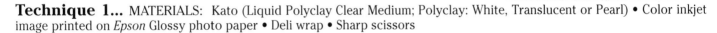

1. Trim image, leaving a border of at least ⅛". **2.** On the image, draw a thin squiggle of Clear Medium. **3.** Spread the medium over the entire image. You don't need a lot of medium, just enough to lightly coat the image. Roll conditioned light colored clay through a medium setting of the pasta machine. Place the clay on a piece of deli paper. Place the image, face down on the clay. Do Not Burnish the image onto the clay. **4.** With a blade, trim and remove excess clay from around the image. **5.** Fold a sheet of deli paper and place the clay and image in the fold.

 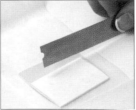   

6. On the same setting of the machine, place the fold of the deli paper between the rollers of the machine. Slowly roll it through the pasta machine. The clay will enlarge beyond the paper. Peel deli paper from the clay. If the clay is sticking to the paper, spray the back of the deli paper with water and it will release. **7.** Trim and remove excess clay around inkjet paper. Bake in the oven at 275°F for 30 minutes. To ensure that the medium has not sealed the edges of the image paper, cut a narrow strip from each side of the cured clay and transfer with scissors. **8-9.** Drop the image into a bowl of water and wait for 30 minutes. The paper can then be peeled from the clay, leaving the image on the clay itself. **10.** If there is any paper residue on the image, wet again and lightly rub to remove. Once the transfer is made, it can be cut with scissors to the desired shape.

continued on pages 6-10

Favorite Pendants   continued from pages 4 - 5

Texture and visual interest are easily added to your polyclay art using rubber stamps or texture sheets. There are 3 techniques for using stamped clay. These are Faux Leaf, Faux Brocade and Faux Silkscreen.

• Faux Leaf requires the paint be applied before the clay is stamped.

• Faux Brocade has a textured surface where the raised stamped portion of clay is colored.

• Faux Silkscreen flattens Faux Brocade.

Have fun making your own delightful creations.

Techniques 2 and 3...

MATERIALS:
Kato Black polyclay • Rubber stamp sheet • *Liquitex* acrylic paint (Red Oxide, Pthalo Green, Iridescent Gold) • *Ranger* Gold Perfect Pearls mica powder • Brush • Spray bottle filled with water

Technique 2: Stamping in Polyclay

To prevent polyclay from sticking to your rubber stamps, you must use a release agent. Release agents include water, Perfect Pearls mica powder and cornstarch (not baby powder or talc). We will use water in a spray bottle.

1. Lay the stamp on your work surface rubber side up. Spray the stamp with water. **2.** Roll clay using a thick setting. Lay the clay on the stamp. Lightly spray the back of the clay with water. **3.** With a roller, apply firm and even pressure, rolling once only from the bottom to the top of the clay sheet. The water applied to the back of the clay prevents the clay from sticking to the rod. **4.** Lift the clay from the stamp and set it aside to dry.

Technique 3: Faux Leaf

Metallic leaf forms no permanent bond with clay. In order to preserve and protect the leaf, it must be glazed after curing. An alternative to metallic leaf is acrylic paint! Once the paint and clay are cured, the paint adheres to the clay and does not require surface treatment to remain permanent. As an added bonus, cane slices may be applied to painted surfaces and will stick.

Acrylic paint "cures" with exposure to air and time. Total curing, depending on the brand of paint, could take days or months. In my experience, Liquitex paint completely cures in approximately 1 week on clay. Clay must be baked before the paint cures or the paint will not stick.

 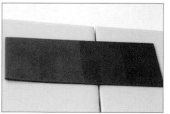 

1. Roll a sheet of Black clay through the thickest setting of the pasta machine. Lightly press it onto a ceramic tile. Dab a light coat of Gold paint onto the clay. Let dry. This should take no more than 15 minutes. **2.** Onto the dry paint, dab another light coat of paint. Repeat until the clay is covered with the paint and the Black has been concealed. Once the paint is dry to the touch, it may be used. Here is a strip of clay showing 1, 2, 3 and 4 light coats of Gold paint.
3. When the paint is dry, slide a blade beneath the clay to release it from the tile.

Technique 4: Faux Silkscreen

Tips: You'll be applying paint onto the surface of raw clay. For easiest application, lightly press the raw clay to a glazed ceramic tile. To remove the clay from the tile, slide a blade beneath the clay, pressing the blade to the surface of the tile and lifting the piece from the blade. For instruction purposes, the clay has been rolled through the thickest setting of a pasta machine – this is recommended for techniques in which the clay will be deeply impressed then rolled thin such as Faux Silkscreen and Faux Brocade.

 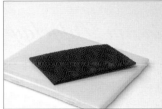 

1. When the water has evaporated from a stamped clay, apply the acrylic paint. Lightly cover your finger with Red Oxide paint. The goal is to dab paint onto the raised areas only. It is best to apply several light coats of paint, building up the color to achieve dense coverage. **2.** Let dry. **3.** Paint must be dry and the roller free of clay residue. Using a thick metal tube, knitting needle or the acrylic rod, roll lightly back and forth one time onto the textured and painted clay. Lift the sheet from your work surface and rotate the sheet 90 degrees. Roll back and forth again. By lifting and rotating the sheet, you will ensure that the pattern stretches evenly in all directions. Continue rolling and rotating the sheet until the surface is flat. It is best to roll many times lightly rather than once or twice heavily.

Technique 5: Faux Brocade

Faux Brocade is a combination of the Faux Leaf, Stamping in Polyclay and Faux Silkscreen.

Begin by making a sheet of Faux Leaf using the thick setting of the pasta machine. Make sure the paint is dry. Lay the stamp on your work surface, rubber side up. Instead of spraying the stamp with water, lightly dust it with Gold Perfect Pearls mica powder which will function as a release agent. Lay the painted clay, paint side down, on the stamp. Lightly spray the back of the clay with water. With the acrylic rod, applying firm and even pressure, roll once only from the bottom to the top of the sheet. You now have a painted and textured sheet of clay.

1. Dab a spotty application of Red Oxide paint to the raised areas of the clay. Colors may be overlayed. **2.** Dab Pthalo Green on areas not covered by the Red Oxide. Let dry. Slide a blade beneath the clay to remove it from the tile. **3.** Using a thick metal tube, knitting needle or the acrylic rod, roll lightly back and forth one time onto the textured and painted clay. Lift the sheet from your work surface and rotate the sheet 90 degrees. Roll back and forth again. By lifting and rotating the sheet, you will ensure that the pattern stretches evenly in all directions. Continue rolling and rotating the sheet until the surface is flat. It is best to roll many times lightly rather than once or twice heavily.

continued on pages 8-10

Favorite Pendants
continued from pages 4 - 7

Technique 6:
Setting and Finishing

MATERIALS:
Kato (Liquid Polyclay Clear Medium; Black polyclay)

1. Roll a medium thin sheet of Black polyclay. Place it on a ceramic tile. Smear a small amount of Clear Medium on the back of the image and press it to the Black clay.

2. How to add 2 Narrow strips of Faux Silkscreen: Clay will distort if you cut a narrow strip and try to move it to the piece, so you must make your second cut while the clay is on the piece. Start by trimming a straight edge in the sheet of Faux Silkscreen. Align the straight edge against the top edge of the clay transfer. Do Not press the sheet to the base Black clay. Cut through the Faux Silkscreen layer only. Leaving the narrow strip in place, lift the Faux Silkscreen sheet from the clay, then remove the blade. Repeat, making a narrow strip against the bottom edge of the clay transfer. **3.** Repeat to add wider strips of Faux Brocade to the top and bottom of the piece.

Favorite Pendants... continued from page 8

4. Cutting through base Black sheet, trim 2 sides straight with blade. Use a flexible blade to trim the top and bottom in a curve. Remove the trimmed pieces. Bake at 275° for 30 minutes. Let cool completely. • Roll a sheet of Black through a medium setting and place it on a ceramic tile. Press any air pockets from between the tile and the clay sheet. Smear a small amount of Clear Medium on the back of the baked piece and press it to the base Black clay. Roll additional Black clay through the second thickest setting of the pasta machine and fold it in half. With an acrylic rod or knitting needle, roll along the fold to expel air and press the layers together. **5.** Cut two ½" wide strips from the folded sheet. These pieces will frame the sides of the piece. When the blade cut through the clay and met your work surface, it formed a sharp corner. That is the side you want facing up so you need to turn each strip over. Align and press the cut edge next to one side of the pendant. If there is gapping, push the clay from the outside of the strip, touching the edge next to the pendant as little as possible. Repeat for the other side.

6. Final shaping: Spray both sides of your blade with water. This will minimize distortion caused by clay sticking to the blade. Cut the arch across the top and bottom leaving a very narrow margin of base clay. Trim the sides of the pendant, removing the excess clay. Bake the piece on the ceramic tile for 45 minutes at 275°. When cool, remove from the tile. **7.** Sanding: With a fine grit sanding block, sand all parts of the Black frame. **8.** Drilling holes for pendant: Drill 1 hole at least ¼" deep in the top of each of the frame pieces. **9.** Adhere cord in holes with Super Glue.

Geisha Card Holder

by Donna Kato

Captivate someone's attention just by taking out your business card? Our Geisha Business Card Case is a guaranteed conversation starter. Make yours in a theme suited to your interests.

Most of us find ordinary business card cases are too small, try using a cigarette case.

MATERIALS:
3" x 4" cigarette case • Kato (Repel gel; Liquid Polyclay Clear Medium; Polyclay blocks: 1 Red, 1 Black) • Liquitex paint (Gold, Red Oxide) • Prepared inkjet transfer • Prepared clay (Faux Leaf, Faux Silkscreen) • Sanding block • Black permanent marking pen • E6000 adhesive

1. Condition clays. (See page 2.) Prepare a mix of Alizarin Crimson using 1 block Red, ¹⁄₁₆ block Black. Lay Black clay on Red clay. Run through the pasta machine until mixed. Cover the top side of the case with a thin sheet of mixed clay. Working from the center, push any air pockets toward the edge to expel them. **2.** Wrap the clay from the top around the corners and down the sides of the case. **3.** Cut clay around latch and hinge. Texture the surface of the clay by pressing with a coarse sanding block.

continued on page 10

Geisha Card Holder
continued from pages 4-9

4. At latch, slide blade between the two sides of the case and cut around. Remove excess clay. If necessary, re-texture areas that might have become flattened by your fingers. Bake the case at 275° for 15 minutes. **5.** Open the case. Slide the blade along the edge of the case to tidy up and cut away any excess clay. **6-7.** With your finger, apply Repel Gel to the edge and then up the sides of the case. Repel Gel will prevent the raw clay you are about to apply from sticking to the baked clay. Let the Repel Gel dry before moving to the next step. With the case closed, cover the bottom side with a thin sheet of clay. Trim the excess clay around the hinge. Open the case and cut the excess clay around the edge. Texture the clay with a coarse sanding block.

8. Finish by trimming the edge with your blade once again. Retexture if necessary. Close the case and bake again for another 45 minutes. • When the case is cool, rinse off the Repel Gel with water.

Decoration: Position the inkjet transfer on the case. Draw around the transfer with a permanent marking pen. Remove transfer. Apply a generous coat of Clear Medium to the area within the drawn box. The Clear Medium will fill in the texture. Press the transfer to the Clear Medium.

Frame Elements: Use Faux Leaf in a combination of Gold and Red Oxide and Faux Silkscreen in Red Oxide on Black clay. You will want to brush a thin coat of Clear Medium where these elements will be applied. Apply thin strips of Faux Leaf around the transfer (see page 6). • Apply Faux Silkscreen elements around the Faux Leaf strips (see page 8.). With a blade, cut the final shape and remove the excess clay. Roll a thin snake of Black clay and wrap around the focal piece. Smooth the clay where the ends of the snake meet. Bake the case for an additional 45 minutes. After the case is cold, loosen the clay at edges and remove the clay covering both sides of the case.• Working one side at a time, apply E6000 along the side of the case. Press the clay back onto the case. Repeat for other side.

Wine Skirt Sets
and
'Sticky Notes' Books

Cathy Johnston

Cathy Johnston

With 23 years of experience working in polymer clay, and 6 years teaching workshops, Cathy is currently doing demonstrations and design work for several companies. Her art has sold at juried craft shows and galleries. Visit her website at

www.cathyjohnston.com.

Making the Front Cover

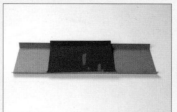

1. First we need to make a tray to use with the Stampress. Cut cardboard 4" x 11". **2.** Score each of the long edges ½" from the edge. Fold up the scored edges. **3** Trace and cut out both templates. Condition and roll out a piece of clay on the second largest setting of the pasta machine. Trim the clay to 4" x 5". Place clay on the cardboard tray from step 1. **4.** Install the stamp wheel in the Stampress.

5. Spritz the clay with a little water. Roll the clay thru the Stampress to impress the image on the clay. **6.** Place the clay, imprint side up, on a sheet of cardboard. Press steel wool on the edges to texture. **7.** Place template A on top of the imprinted clay. Trim around the template. Remove the template and excess clay. **8.** Place plastic wrap on top of the trimmed clay and smooth the edges with your finger. Remove the plastic and set aside.

'Sticky Notes' Books

by Cathy Johnston

Small enough to fit in your pocket, purse, or cell phone carrier, these handy little books can be made to fit anyone's style.

MATERIALS:
Kato Polyclay (Green, Yellow, Brown) • 2" x 3" Sticky Notepad • 3¼" x 5½" book cloth • 4" x 11" cardboard • Templates (A Top, B Bottom) • *Clearsnap* (Stampress, Rollagraph Botanical Tiles stamp wheel; ColorBox Olive Pastel Fluid Chalk ink) • *Delta* Ceramcoat Black antiquing gel • Bone Folder • Synthetic steel wool • ½" stiff bristled paintbrush • 60 grit sandpaper • Deli paper • Heat gun • Craft knife • Plastic wrap • Rag • Spray bottle • *Mainely Shades* lampshade glue • Double-stick carpet tape

Making the Back Cover

9. Apply glue to the sticky edge of the notepad. Set aside to dry. Roll a piece of clay on the 2nd largest setting of the pasta machine. Press the steel wool pad against clay to texture. **10.** Set this clay on a piece of cardboard with the textured side down. Place Template B on the clay. Roll out some more clay on the thickest setting. **11.** Cut and stack the clay for a double thickness. Trim one edge. Place beside Template B. **12.** Ink notepad edges.

Assembling the Book

 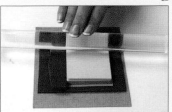  

13. Split the notepad in half. Save one half for another book. Place one half on Template B. **14.** Roll across the clay and notepad to adhere the clay to the back cover. **15.** Place Template A on top of the notepad and align the dashed line on template A with the left edge of the notepad. **16.** Use a Nu-Blade to trim the left edge of Template A. Remove Template A and notepad.

continued on page 14

17. Trim around the top, right and bottom edges of Template B. Remove template. **18.** Texture the spine edge with steel wool. Put the plastic over the back cover and smooth the edges with your finger. Remove plastic. Bake the cover and the base of the book at 275° for 30-45 minutes. Let cool. Antique the covers with Black antiquing gel. Let set 10 minutes, then wipe off with excess gel with a rag. **19.** Use the cover as a guide to fold the book cloth. Use a bone folder to burnish the fold in the book cloth. **20.** Ink the book cloth.

21. Heat set the ink with a heat gun. **22.** Sand the inside of the cover so the glue adheres to the book cover. **23.** Apply glue to the sanded side of the cover. Place a piece of deli paper or scrap paper in the fold of the book cloth. Spread glue out to the edges of the book cloth. **24.** Place the cover onto the book cloth, aligning the folded edge with the left side of the front cover.

25. Use the bone folder to crease the folds. **26.** Trim the book cloth with a craft knife. **27.** Put some carpet tape on the back of the notepad. **28.** Remove the backing from the tape and place this in your new book.

Template

A

Cover

Template

B

Back

Wine Skirt Sets

by Cathy Johnston

These wine skirts are an attractive way to identify your wine glass at a party. This great gift contains 4 skirts in a stylish gift box. Cheers!

Wine Skirt Preparation

1. Trace and cut out the template for the wine skirt.

2. Condition clay, see page 2.

3. See Recipe to mix colors or select four colors you prefer.

4. Roll out a piece of clay on the #6 or #7 setting.

5. Cut a 3" x 3" square of each of the 4 mixed colors.

Recipes for Colors:

Gold: 4 parts Yellow, 1 part Brown
Red: 1 part Red, 1 part Brown
Yellow - Orange: 4 parts Orange, 3 parts Brown
Green: 5 parts Yellow, 1 part Green, 2 parts Brown

Wine Skirt

BASIC MATERIALS:
Kato (Liquid Polyclay Clear Medium; Polyclay: Red, Green, Yellow, Orange, Brown) • *The Stamp Barn* Leaf cube • *Clearsnap* ColorBox Fluid Chalk inks (Dark Brown, Yellow Cadmium, Burnt Sienna, Dark Moss, Deep Green) • Four 4" x 5" pieces of cardboard • Synthetic steel wool • 400 Grit sandpaper
MATERIALS FOR SKIRT:
2½" round cookie cutter • *Kemper* round cutter (¾") • Clay blade • Plastic wrap • *Style Stones* brush

1. Place each square of clay on a piece of cardboard. Press a steel wool pad against the clay to texture and remove air bubbles between clay and cardboard.
2. Stamp each of the four clay squares. Don't use too much pressure or the clay might rip.

3. Place the 2½" round cutter onto the clay and press firmly. **4.** Remove the extra clay from the outer edges of the cutter. **5.** Carefully lift the cutter off the clay. If the clay pulls away from the cardboard use the steel wool pad to gently reposition the clay. • Gently place the skirt template on the clay. Trace the center hole with a needle tool. **6.** Use the ¾" cutter to punch out the center. Remove the clay from the center.

continued on page 16-17

Wine Skirt Sets
continued from page 14

7. Slice the wine skirt from the center to the edge of the skirt. **8.** To make sure there are no air bubble between the clay and the cardboard, texture gently with the steel wool pad. Bake the wine skirts at 275° for 30 minutes. Let cool. **9.** Lightly sand the edges if needed. **10.** Color the stamp images with an inking brush. Return the skirts to the oven and bake for 5 minutes at 275° to heat set the ink.

Wine Skirts Gift Case
by Cathy Johnston
This great gift contains 4 skirts in a stylish gift box. Cheers!

BASIC MATERIALS:
Kato (Liquid Polyclay Clear Medium; Polyclay: Red, Green, Yellow, Orange, Brown) • *The Stamp Barn* Leaf cube • *Clearsnap* ColorBox Fluid Chalk inks (Dark Brown, Yellow Cadmium, Burnt Sienna, Dark Moss, Deep Green) • Synthetic steel wool • 400 Grit sandpaper
MATERIALS FOR GIFT CASE:
9" of White elastic ¹⁄₁₆" cord • Template of cover • Tracing paper • 4½" x 6½" cardstock • *Golden* Matte Varnish • 2 clothespins or binder clips • Bone folder • 6" wire 28 gauge • *Style Stones* Inking Brushes • 1" foam brush • *Kemper* round cutters (⁷⁄₁₆", ½") • ¹⁄₁₆" drill bit • *Crafter's Pick* Incredibly Tacky glue • *Loctite* Super Glue Gel

    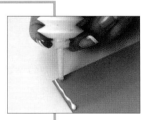

PREPARATION FOR GIFT CASE: Score and fold cardstock to 3¼" x 4½". Open. Score and fold a line 1¼" in from the long side. This will form the inside pocket. Open flat.
1. Drag an inkpad across the outside of the cardstock case. Let dry. **2.** Stamp the outside of the case. **3.** Color the stamped images with a small stiff brush. With your index finger apply Clear Medium to the outside of the case. Let this sit for a couple of minutes so it self levels out. Bake for 15 minutes at 275°. Let cool **4.** Apply a second coat if you want to make the case sturdier. If desired, apply a coat of Matte Varnish to take the glossy finish off the Clear Medium. **5.** Glue the inside edges of the case, fold up the bottom flap to form a pocket.

Wine Skirt Template
2½" Outside Dia.
¾" Inside Dia.

Score and Fold

Template for Wine Skirt Case

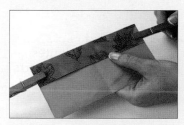   

6. Clamp glued pocket until it dries. **7.** Condition clay. Roll out clay on the thickest setting of the pasta machine. Cut out 2 circles with the ½" cutter. Roll each into a ball. Shape into teardrop and slightly flatten. **8.** Use a drilling motion with the needle tool to drill a hole halfway into larger end of each teardrop. **9.** Place plastic wrap over leftover clay. Cut a ½" circle. Use the cutter to cut the hole completely out of the clay.

10. Remove plastic wrap. **11.** Use the $\frac{7}{16}$" cutter and make a slight indent in the ½" circle. **12.** Now you have a button bead. Make two more button beads. **13.** With the needle tool, drill a hole into the center of each button bead. Bake for 30 minutes at 275°. Let cool.

14. Pull elastic cord across a stamp pad to color the cord to match the case or beads. **15-17.** Redrill halfway into each of the baked teardrop beads.

18. Apply a dab of glue gel on one end of the elastic cord. Place this end into the flattened teardrop bead. Repeat with the other end of the elastic cord. **19.** Redrill the center of the button. **20.** Fold the wire in half. Place the elastic cord into the fold of the wire. **21.** Thread the wire from the front of the button into the hole of the button and pull this thru the hole. Insert wine skirts into the pocket of the case. Wrap case with elastic cord.

Millefiori Flowers
Mokume Gane Jewelry
Leaf Pendant

Judy Belcher

Judy Belcher

Judy's art has been juried into national exhibitions and is sold through galleries across the country. She is the author of the book Polymer Clay Creative Traditions. Judy has been a frequent guest artist for the Carol Duvall Show (HGTV, DIY) and Beads, Baubles and Jewels (PBS). Visit her website at

www.judybelcherdesigns.com

Tip: All the flowers (pages 18-21) are all constructed the same way. The ganes are constructed differently to create different color petals.

Flower with Blended Petals

by Judy Belcher

Once I got started making these flowers, I just couldn't quit! I kept manipulating the cane to see just how many different looking flowers I could make using a variety of Millefiori cane techniques all based on that wonderful Skinner Blend.

MATERIALS: Kato (Clear Liquid Medium; Polyclay: ½ block Magenta, ½ block White) • *Forsline* Clay Shaper • Pin back

1. Roll out each color of clay on the thickest setting of pasta machine. Cut triangles of each color and put them together to form a 3½" square. **2.** See page 3 to turn this square into a Skinner Blend. Thin the sheet until the blend is very long. **3.** Roll up the sheet, beginning with White edge to form a blended bulls eye cane. Compress and reduce the cane slightly. **4.** Cut 10 thin slices from the cane.

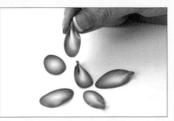

5. Place the slices on the pasta machine lined up across the roller. Roll the slices through the pasta machine on a very thin setting to form the flower petals. **6.** Pinch one end of each petal and place pinched ends together to begin forming the flower. **7.** Form the flower by joining five petals in the center. **8.** Add another layer of five petals, slightly offsetting each petal.

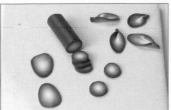

9. Gently compress the center with the blunt end of a clay shaper. **10.** Reduce the remaining cane by rolling and stretching. Cut 7 thin slices from this cane. Roll the slices through the pasta machine on a very thin setting to form the flower petals. • Pinch one end of each petal. **11.** Add to the flower center. • Bake the flower for 20 minutes at 275°. **12.** Adhere a pin back with Liquid Clay. For added strength and a nice finished look, adhere a clay slice over the pin back. Bake for 20 minutes at 275°.

continued on pages 20-21

Flowers

continued from pages 18-19

1. Use the blended jellyroll cane from the Flower with Blended Petals on page 19. Prior to slicing the cane, use a thin knitting needle to form ridges down one side of the cane. This makes each petal have a ruffled edge.

2. To form the smaller petals, try cutting the slices thinner. **3-4.** Follow steps on page 19 to assemble the flower.

Ruffle Edge Flower

Perfect petals form an irresistible flower.

MATERIALS: Kato (Clear Liquid Medium; Polyclay: ½ block Magenta, ½ block White) • *Forsline* Clay Shaper • Thin knitting needle • Pin back

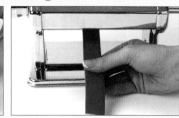

Flower with Striped Petals

Tiny stripes create a striking bold flower.

1. Use the blended jellyroll cane from the Flower with Blended Petals on page 19. Compress the cane to form a flattened overall shape. **2.** Roll the cane through the pasta machine on the thickest setting.

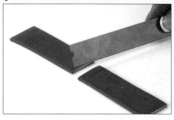

3. Cut the resulting thin cane into two equal pieces.
4. Stack the pieces and roll through the pasta machine.

MATERIALS: Kato (Clear Liquid Medium; Polyclay: ½ block Magenta, ½ block White) • *Forsline* Clay Shaper • Pin back

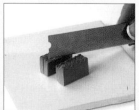

5. Repeat until the desired striped cane is formed. Stack the sheets to form a cane ½" high. **6.** Cut the stack in half. **7.** With the cut edges down, adhere the pieces together. **8.** Compress into a petal shape. **9.** Follow steps on page 19 to assemble the flower.

Millefiori means "thousand flowers" in Italian. The process is an ancient glass technique. Millefiori cane work lends itself very well to polymer clay. The cane is formed by piecing the clay together like a puzzle. The cane is then carefully compressed to reduce the size and, therefore, the image of the cane. The resulting cane can be sliced to form beads or shaped into delicate decorative petals.

These flowers are made using many of the same steps as the Flower with Blended Petals, page 19. You are going to love the light, airy feel of these delicate flowers.

Flower with Wavy Striped Petals

This flower can be more than a pretty pin. Use it to decorate a box or frame, give it as a gift, or add a stem and keep it in a vase.

MATERIALS: Kato (Clear Liquid Medium; Polyclay: ½ block Magenta, ½ block White) • *Forsline* Clay Shaper • Pin back

1. Begin with the same right triangles for a Skinner Blend. See Step 1 of the Flower with Blended Petals on p. 19. **2.** Only roll through the pasta machine five times. **3.** Cut the resulting sheet into six equal sections, making sure each section contains both colors. **4.** Stack these sections into a loaf, varying the edges slightly.

5. Compress the loaf into a square. Go ahead and compress quickly, for the resulting wavy lines make the petals more interesting. **6.** Compress the cane into a petal shape. **7.** Slice cane and run the pieces through the pasta machine with the White ends touching the roller. **8.** Pinch the White end to form the petals. Follow steps on page 19 to assemble the flower.

Variation

1. For another variation, place the cane slices on the pasta machine roller White side up. Pinch the Magenta end to form the petals. **2.** Follow steps on page 19 to assemble the flower.

Leaf Pod Purse Pendant

by Judy Belcher

Delicate shaped leaves elegantly cover a small purse for a stunning pendant reminiscent of Victorian beaded bags.

MATERIALS:
Kato (Clear Liquid Medium; Polyclay: ½ block Violet, ½ block White, ⅓ block Black)
• *Fire Mountain Gems* Heart shaped Filigree Purse

1. Roll out each color of clay on the thickest setting. Cut triangles of each color 2" wide x 4½" tall. **2.** Put them together to form a rectangle. Prepare a Skinner Blend. (See page 3.) **3.** Lay the sheet of blended clay so the White edge is to one side and the Violet to the other. Tightly roll up the blended sheet to form a log.

4. Turn the log up on its end and compress downward. **5.** Cut the log in half while it is still up on its end. This will result in two half circle logs or canes. While the half circle cane is up on its end, slice it into 3 sections to form the veins of the leaf. Repeat with the other half circle cane. **6.** Roll out a sheet of Black clay on a relatively thin setting. Insert thin strips of the Black clay between the cut sections. **7.** Squeeze all the pieces back together to reform the blended log.

Change the clay colors in the Leaf Pod project for a dazzling collection with a different look.

The bracelet bangle and matching earrings are sure to receive as many compliments as the leafy pendant.

Leaf Jewelry

Better than anything you will find in the boutique, you will love wearing your own line of designer jewelry. The filigree purse comes in a variety of shapes.

For earrings, press 4 leaves together. Pierce a hole in the top of the leaf for the earring finding. After baking, attach finding with a jump ring. Adhere leaves to a purchased bangle to make the bracelet. Tip: Before decorating it, test the purchased bracelet to ensure it will not melt in the oven.

8. Continue compressing and rolling until the cane is ½" in diameter and 6" long. **9.** Wrap the entire outside of the cane with a thin sheet of Black clay. Cut the cane into twelve ½" segments. Keep each segment in line, as we will be cutting the cane paying special attention to the gradation of color. **10.** Look at each end of each segment. Pinch each cane to form a leaf. **11.** Keeping the leaf segments in order, cut 10 thin slices from each cane.

12. Beginning at the bottom of the purse, press only the top of the the leaf into the filigree work. • Complete the purse row by row, overlapping the tips of the leaves with the tops from the row before. **13.** By keeping the leaf slices in order, the blend will become apparent as the leaves are added to the purse. Cover the front, sides and half of the back of the purse, but not the flap. Bake the purse for 15 minutes at 275°.

Allow the purse to cool and continue covering the purse. This allows you to handle the purse more easily without distorting the layers. **14.** Continue adding cane slices to the flap of the purse. To insure that the flap remains secure, open the purse and squeeze a thin layer of Clear Liquid Medium onto the filigree work of the back of the flap and bake for 30 minutes at 275° degrees. **15.** Add a chain or ribbon to complete the purse.

Turquoise Splendor

by Judy Belcher

Make your own Mokume Gane jewelry in your favorite colors. Add earring findings, necklace chains, or pin backs for your own sparkling, colorful collection.

Mokume Gane

Mokume Gane is an ancient Japanese metalsmithing technique. By laminating different metals the sword was strengthened and an interesting pattern was created when the weapon was forged and filed. Mokume Gane polymer clay techniques involve thin layers of clay that are manipulated in some way, then shaved off to reveal the pattern. My favorite approach uses a rubber stamp which reveals a more deliberate pattern.

Silver Beading Discs are a wonderful way to display polymer clay. One of the problems that polymer clay artists have had in the past was how to adhere the clay to a flat Silver surface. Most pendants outlive the adhesives in the settings. The loops of the beading discs create a surface for the clay to grasp permanently. Using Silver leaf in the stamped pattern of the clay unites the clay and sterling Silver beautifully, for a simply stunning creation.

Turquoise Splendor

MATERIALS:
Kato (Clear Liquid Medium; Polyclay: ⅛ block Turquoise, ⅛ block White, ⅛ block Violet) • *Fire Mountain Gems* Hill Tribe Silver beading disc • *Houston Arts* Silver Leaf • *Clearsnap* Waves and Weaves Molding Mat • 1" circle cookie cutter • Plastic wrap • Spray bottle with water

1. Roll out each color of clay on a relatively thin setting. Cut clay 1" x 1½". **2.** Stack the sheets together: Turquoise, White, Violet. **3.** Roll the stack through the pasta machine again on a thicker setting. Roll again at a thinner setting. Roll again on the thinnest setting. **4.** Cut the sheet in half.

5. Stack one on top of the other. **6.** Roll these sheets again through the thinnest setting.

7. Cut the sheet into thirds. **8.** Press Silver leaf onto two of the sheets of clay.

9. Stack the sheets, one on top of the other with a layer of Silver leaf between each sheet: Clay, Silver leaf, Clay, Silver leaf, Clay. **10.** Cut the stack in half and flip over one half to form a two color surface. Lay the clay on a ceramic tile. You want the clay to stick to the surface.

Turquoise & Silver

Design a beautiful and elegant jewelry set. The beading discs come in a variety of shapes and sizes.

Coral Swirls

Create your own colors and swirls in your favorite colors... necklace pendants and earrings.

11. Spray the texture sheet with a fine mist of water. Lay the texture sheet down against the clay. **12.** Firmly roll the clay to deeply impress the texture into the clay. Roll across the surface one time only or the image may blur.

continued on page 26

13. Allow clay to stick to the surface of the ceramic tile. **14.** Carefully shave off just the raised areas of the clay with a very sharp blade. Work in small areas of the sheet. Try not to cut too deeply, as some of each of the colors of clay and Silver leaf must remain to form the pattern. Bending the blade as you slice might be easier for you.
15. Roll the finished sheet through the pasta machine beginning with the thickest setting. Reset the pasta machine to incrementally thinner settings and continue rolling the sheet through it until the sheet is smooth.
16. Roll out a sheet of Violet clay on the thickest setting.

17. Carefully stack the patterned sheet of clay to the Violet clay using the acrylic rod to work out any air that might get trapped under the layer. **18.** Lay a sheet of plastic wrap over the surface of the clay and stretch so that no wrinkles are present. Choose a nicely decorated part of the clay and press the circle cookie cutter straight down into the clay. Remove the plastic wrap. Notice the nicely beveled edges. **19.** Roll out 3 tiny logs of leftover clay. **20.** Place each log of clay through the beading loops of the Silver disc.

21. Press the finished piece onto the loops and firmly onto the clay logs. **22.** Turn the disc over and press the clay firmly on a clean sheet of typing paper on the table top. This will smooth the surface of the pendant. Bake for 30 minutes at 275°. Let cool. **23.** To keep the Silver leaf from tarnishing, place a few drops of Clear Liquid Medium on the clay pendant and spread in a circular motion with your finger. Bake again for 10 minutes at 275°.
24. Remove the pendant from the oven and allow to cool. Buff lightly on your jeans or with a cotton rag.

Majestic Beads
Leaf Earrings
Klew

Klew

Karen Lewis (aka Klew) found polymer clay in the late 80's. Although Klew's clay choices have changed over time, today she prefers Kato Polyclay, and the excitement has kept its momentum for her. Her art has been published in over 8 trade magazines and 10 books. She has 5 instructional videos to round out her portfolio. Find out more about her work at

www.klewexpressions.com

Majestic Beads

by KLEW

I wanted to give you something as magnificent and enchanting as you are, something treasured for its uniqueness and beauty. Create a magical moment when you give a necklace of handmade beads.

MATERIALS:

Kato Polyclay (3 oz. White, 3 oz. Purple, 1 oz. Beige for side veins, 2 oz. Black, 2 oz. Metallic Green for the center, 2 oz. Metallic Gold for outer wrap)

BASIC POLYTOOLS:

Pasta Machine, flexible steel scraper tool, needle tool, tissue blade, Corian work surface.

TIP: Bake to manufacturer's instructions on the package, a minimum of 20 minutes.

KLEW'S TIPS

TIP: Vein thickness is relative to the circumference of your log, so keep in mind that if you don't have far to reduce something, then you may want to make your veins even thinner!

TIP: As you are creating your leaf cane, slice off a sample like I've done for the photos here and it will be easier to remember the next time you make one.

TIP: Always look at the end of your cane and hold it at arm's length to decide whether you like the colors together. Also check to be sure that the lines are thin enough, etc.

TIP: The famous Skinner blend takes so many passes through the pasta machine that I like to make a good amount of it!

TIP: When you make a small rectangle or square of opposing triangles for the blend and they are not the full width of the rollers, and the clay eventually travels to fill the width, then your clay shrinks in height which is hard to do the folding thing!

TIP: If you use lighter colors for the leaves, you can use black for all the veins.

TIP: If yours didn't come out the way you like, you still have the other two halves to try again.

"Leaf - Cane ala Klew". **1.** Make 2 Skinner blends and roll each into a log, one with the White clay on the inside, one with Purple clay on the inside. See page 3. For illustration purposes, the pictures show slices from the rolls, not the whole roll. **2.** Stand each roll on end, slice them vertically down the middle to make 2 semicircle halves. Swap one half with the other and join, but not too well as you will be slicing them apart. **3.** Stand this cylinder on end and make three slices running at a diagonal across the shades. **4.** For the veins, roll out a sheet of Beige on a thin setting. Take one section of the Skinner blend and place it firmly cut side down onto the sheet of Beige. Trim around each section of the blend. Carefully use blade to lift clay from your work surface and re-assemble. **5.** Carefully slice down through the middle so one side shades light to dark and the other shades dark to light.

6. Flip one side so the veins are at right angles to each other. • For the center vein, roll out 1 thin sheet of Black (double diameter of center of leaf) and a medium thickness sheet the size of the center diameter of Metallic Green. Place Green to one end of Black sheet and fold Black over to sandwich it in. Pinch the fold sharply. Fit inside both halves of leaf cane and trim to fit. **7.** For the outer wrap, roll out a sheet of Metallic Green on a medium thin setting. Trim to fit the length of your log. Wrap and smooth the seams. Roll out a medium thin sheet of Black for the last layer. Trim to fit the length of your log. Wrap and smooth the seams, rolling gently without lengthening the roll. **8.** Look at the end. With your index finger and thumb, gently pinch the side with the veins pointing up. Repeat at other end. Straighten log if needed. With index finger and thumb, pinch all three sides to create a triangle shaped cylinder. Smooth out your finger prints with a stroking, dragging motion with your thumb and forefinger along the corners against the table, not the top. This will keep the top edges from getting too thin. Continue until the cane is 3 times its original length. Flip occasionally to prevent the ends from becoming too thick and the middle too thin. If the ends do not reduce at the same rate, simply take a few minutes to pinch them down without stretching the middle to get them the same size as the rest of the cane. **9.** Once you have it reduced to about a ¾" diameter, it is time to pinch the bottom two corners together to form your leaf shape. It will take several passes all along the cane to do this and you may want to cut your cane in half if it is too long to handle. Don't do any trimming yet. Take 3 passes of pinching to pull the sides together without tearing. If it starts to tear, gently push the clay back together and continue. Once it is all pinched together along the bottom of the leaf, the cane will be a bit curled. Just lay it on the table and gently run your fingers along the length a few times to straighten.

10. With the point of the leaf toward the ceiling, gently grasp the point. Lightly press against the table in a rocking stroking motion to smooth out the bottom seam. Cut it in half again to reveal your creation! **11.** Slice and shape. Use leaves for earrings or beads. **12.** Make some thicker slices and gently pinch into a natural sculpted shape.

Add Leaves to Make Large Beads

To make beads, roll out some clay into balls. Apply leaf slices, and roll smooth. Shape bead after the leaves are rolled in smooth. Pierce with a needle tool. **13.** You can also shape the base bead first and then add sculpted leaves. Bake following the manufacturers instructions, a minimum of 20 minutes.

Dangle Earrings

MATERIALS NEEDED:

Kato Polyclay (3 oz. white, 3 oz. color, 1 oz. light color for side veins, 2 oz. black, 2 oz. of color for the center and outer wrap).

Attach clay leaves to tiny chains and beads to make beautiful earrings.

Gail Ritchey

Gail is a polymer clay design-er and author of "Making Miniature Villages' in Polymer Clay. She is Grand Prize winner of FIMO's Jetting to Germany Contest and has written clay articles for art and jewelry magazines.. Gail is on the CHA Designer Council. Visit

www.cottagefever.com.

Heart Pendant

MATERIALS: Heart cookie cutter • Black beading wire • Black rubber tubing • 2 crimp beads • Clasp • Knitting needle

Earrings

MATERIALS: Earring backs • Flower cookie cutter
INSTRUCTIONS: Secure earring backs on colored clay with Liquid Clay. Cover with thin Black clay, trim and bake.

Rectangular Pendant

MATERIALS: Flat assorted Black beads • Clasp • Black bead-ing wire • 2 crimp beads • Needle tool
INSTRUCTIONS: Follow 1-5 below using a double thickness of backing clay. Run a beading wire through the hole in the pendant. String beads. Attach a clasp with crimp beads.

Crackled Jewelry

by Gail Ritchey

Create textured jewelry with polymer clay that has been crackled. This is not a painted crackle finish, but actual crackled clay.

GENERAL MATERIALS:
Kato (Black Polyclay; Liquid Polyclay Clear Medium)
• *Jacquard* Pearl-Ex (True Blue, Spring Green, Red Russet)
• Heat gun • Polyester batting • Craft knife • *Loew Cornell* Brushes (wash, mini mop)

1. Condition Black clay. Roll one half of the Black clay on the thickest setting of your pasta machine. Place it on a tile. Using the heat gun, heat the top of the clay until the clay surface turns dull. Do not heat too long or you will bake the sheet.

2. Immediately run the slicing blade under the sheet to remove it from the tile. Reduce the thickness on the pasta machine by one, then run the sheet through the pasta machine. Reduce the setting by one again, turn the sheet 90° and run it through. Repeat not turning. **3.** With your fingers or the mini mop brush, apply colors of powders. **4.** Cut the shape. Place on a batting covered ceramic tile. Bake at 275° for 30 minutes. **5.** Run the remainder of the Black clay on the thickest setting. Place the baked shape on the sheet, trim around the shape with a craft knife. Smooth the edges. **6.** Thin a piece of Black clay on medium thin setting. **7.** Cut two ½" x 1" strips. Place the knitting needle on the back of the heart. Brush the ends of the strips with Clear Medium and place over the knitting needle. Bake the shape on the same tile for 60 minutes. Coat the front of the shape with a thin coating of Clear Medium. Bake again for 20 minutes. **8.** Run wire thru rubber tubing. String on heart. Attach clasp with crimp beads.

Confetti Frame, Fabulous Pendant, Bookmark and Art Journal
Kim Cavender

Kim Cavender

Kim is a full-time polymer clay artist and designer. She travels frequently to teach and demonstrate the exciting medium of polymer clay at workshops and trade shows across the country. She has been a guest of HGTV's The Carol Duvall Show and is the author of Polymer Clay For the Fun of It. Kim's work and teaching schedule can be seen at

www.kimcavender.com.

Rainbow Confetti Photo Frame

by Kim Cavender

Polymer clay makes it so easy to turn a dull, boring frame into one that's exploding with color and fun. The only hard part of this project is trying to decide which photo you'd like to display in your fabulous new frame!

MATERIALS:
Kato (Liquid Clay; Polyclay: Black, White, Yellow, Orange, Red, Magenta, Violet, Turquoise, Green) • Smooth-sided photo frame • *Kemper* circle cutters (⅜", ⅝", ¾") • Paintbrush for use with Liquid Clay • Craft knife • Disposable foam brush • Texture tool (60 grit sandpaper or *Scotch-Brite* scrubbing pad) • *Sobo* White glue • Small ceramic tile • Clay blade

Tip: Choose a smooth-sided frame that can easily be covered with clay. Mine is wood but you can also use frames made from metal or glass with good results. If you're unsure about the frame's ability to withstand the heat of the oven, remove the glass and easel back and bake it at 275° before applying any clay.

   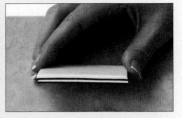

1. Brush a thin layer of glue on the front and sides of the frame. Allow the glue to dry until clear. **2.** Condition and roll the Black clay on a medium thin setting on the pasta machine. Cover one side of the frame at a time, taking care not to trap air bubbles under the clay. Smooth the seams where the Black clay strips meet and trim away the excess clay. Bake the covered frame at 275° for 30 minutes. Allow to cool. **3.** Roll a sheet of White clay through the pasta machine at a medium setting and trim this sheet to 3" x 4". Repeat this step with a sheet of Black clay. Place the White sheet on top of the Black, smoothing it into place with your fingers to avoid trapping air bubbles. **4.** Cut this rectangle in half and stack again. You should now have a stack with 4 different layers.

5. Cut the block in half and stack two more times, always stacking Black on top of White. Press gently to adhere the layers together. Use a clay blade to trim away any uneven edges. **6.** Cut thin slices from the side of the striped stack and use the clay blade to cut small strips from these slices. Set these aside. **7.** Condition ¼ package each of Yellow, Orange, Red, Magenta, Violet, Turquoise, and Green clays at the thickest setting on your pasta machine. Cut each color into a large triangle and arrange them as shown. Follow the instructions for completing a Skinner blend (see page 3). The completed blend will have a rainbow look to it. **8.** Thin the blend by running it through the pasta machine at progressively thinner settings with all colors touching the rollers. Don't fold the blend. Thin it to a medium setting. Trim away the uneven edges and begin rolling the blend up from one multicolored edge to another.

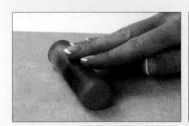   

9. Compress the log by rolling it back and forth on your work surface. As you roll, your hands should be exerting pressure from the ends of the log inward towards the center. Occasionally stop and gently roll the center to keep the log smooth. Continue compressing until you have a log about 2"-3" long. **10.** Cut a thick slice from the rainbow-colored log and run it through the pasta machine with all colors touching the rollers. Continue to roll the blend through until it's very thin. Place the thinned sheet of clay on a ceramic tile, smoothing carefully to prevent trapping air bubbles under the clay. Lightly texture the rainbow sheet with the 60 grit sandpaper. **11.** Use the cutters to punch out three different sizes of circles to embellish your frame. Remove the excess clay and lift the circles from the tile by sliding your clay blade underneath them. **12.** Brush a thin coat of Liquid Clay on the covered frame and arrange the rainbow circles around the frame in groups of 3. Fill in any spaces with the small strips you cut from the Black and White striped stack. Press gently to adhere them. Bake the frame at 275° for 30 minutes. Allow to cool.

Art Journal and Bookmark

by Kim Cavender

What better way to keep track of all those inspiring thoughts and ideas than in your very own art journal? Just for fun, make a matching bookmark. Both the bookmark and the clay journal covers need to be both very strong and flexible. I recommend using Kato Polyclay to ensure a successful and long-lasting project.

1. Remove the front and back covers from the notebook by slightly bending the wire coils. These covers will become the templates for the polymer clay covers you'll create. **2.** Mix ¾ of a package each of Violet, Magenta, and Red clays with a quarter-sized ball of Pearl clay. Use a #3 setting on the pasta machine(Atlas brand) to roll a sheet a little larger than the journal cover. Place it on a ceramic tile, smoothing carefully to avoid trapping air bubbles. Texture the clay lightly with the linen texture sheet. Lay the front cover of the notebook on top of the textured clay sheet and trim around it. **3.** Use a needle tool or toothpick to mark the placement of the holes for the spiral binding. Remove the template and use the ⁵⁄₁₆" circle cutter to make the holes on the left side of the front cover. Remove the excess clay from the holes using a needle tool or toothpick. • Repeat for the back cover. Remember to make the holes for the spiral binding on the right side of the back cover. Set the unbaked covers aside, but don't remove them from the ceramic tiles. **4.** Mix ¼ package each of Green, Gold and Pearl clay with a dime-sized ball of Red clay to get the Green color shown. Mix ¼ package each of Green, Turquoise, and Pearl clay with a dime-sized ball of Orange clay to get the Blue color shown. Make a Skinner blend with these two colors. (See page 3.) Roll the blend on a thin setting and place it on a ceramic tile, taking care not to trap air bubbles under the clay. Lightly texture the blended clay sheet by pressing with 60 grit sandpaper. Stamp your images onto the Skinner blend using the Archival ink. Press hard enough to transfer the ink, but not so hard that you distort the clay. I lined up several images to form a bookmark shape. Detailed cutting of the stamped images will be made after baking. Bake the stamped images on the ceramic tile at 275° for 20 minutes.

MATERIALS:

Kato (Liquid Polyclay; Polyclay: Violet, Magenta, Red, Pearl, Green, Turquoise, Gold, Orange, Black) • 6" x 8" purchased notebook or journal with removable covers • Black waxed linen cord • 6 small Black grommets • 3 hinged metal clamps • Assorted beads • *Invoke Arts* rubber stamps (Plain Jane Paper Doll, Artpost I, Textures I & II, Whimsical Borders, Artquotes I, Collage Words I, Artphrases 2, Dream Face Blocks, Imagine Tag) • *Ranger* (Jet Black Archival inkpad, Distress Peeled Paint inkpad) • *Shade-tex* Linen texture sheet • *Kemper* 5/16" circle cutter • *Fiskars* 1/8" circle punch • 3 ceramic tiles 7" x 9" • Needle tool or toothpick • Small paintbrush dedicated to liquid clay • 60 grit sandpaper • Polybonder glue • Craft knife

5. Allow them to cool slightly. It will be easier to cut the images if they're slightly warm. Keeping the clay on the warm tile, use a craft knife to cut carefully around the stamped images. Use a 1/8" circle punch to punch a hole in the top of the bookmark and holes in the doll where indicated by the rubber stamps. Brush a little Polybonder glue onto the grommets and insert them into the holes you punched in the doll. Let the glue dry. **6.** Brush a little Liquid Clay on the back of the stamped images and place them on the front and back covers as shown. Press gently to adhere them to the clay covers. Roll a few thin snakes and tiny balls of Black clay and arrange them on the front cover as shown. Bake the covers on the ceramic tiles at 275 degrees for 30 minutes. Let them cool.

7. Clip the notebook pages together using the metal clamps and slide the pages off the metal coil. Remove only one metal clamp at a time and use the Distress ink pad to ink around the edges of the pages. Let the ink dry and keep the metal clamps in place. Reassemble the notebook by placing the back cover onto the metal coil. Add the notebook pages and remove the metal clamps. Finally, replace the front cover. **8.** To complete the bookmark, cut 2 lengths of waxed linen cord 10" long. Fold the cords in half and insert the folded loops through the hole in the top of the bookmark. Pull the 4 ends of the cord through the loops to secure the cord. String assorted beads and small stamped and baked clay charms onto the ends of the cords. Thread the cord ends back through the last 2 or 3 beads and tie a knot to secure the beads and charms. Trim the excess cord.

MATERIALS:
Kato (Liquid Polyclay; Polyclay: White, Black, Yellow, Brown, Turquoise, Green) • *AMACO* Moon push mold • 6" Silver 18 gauge wire • 24" buna $\frac{1}{16}$" cord • #5 O-ring • *Zettiology* Word set rubber stamp • *Craf-T Products* Decorating chalks • *Clearsnap* Olive pigment inkpad • *Kemper* pro needle tool • Toothpicks • Paint brushes (Shader, small brush for Liquid Clay) • Cornstarch • 60 grit sandpaper • Polyester batting • Index cards • Jewelry pliers • Wire cutters • Hand-held drill • Polybonder glue • Acrylic rod • Clay blade

1. Mix a package of White clay with pea-sized balls of Brown and Yellow clay to make an Off-White color. Roll out clay at the thickest setting. Cut 2 rectangles 1¼" x 2½". Lightly texture one side of each rectangle with the 60 grit sandpaper.

Fabulous Face Pendant

by Kim Cavender

If you like uncommon things, this is a pendant you're sure to wear over and over again. The wonderful mold designed by polymer clay artist Maureen Carlson makes it easy to create a truly impressive piece of jewelry and the adjustable closure makes it perfect for any type of neckline.

2. Turn one rectangle over, textured side down, onto a clean index card. Use pliers to bend one end of the Silver wire into a zig-zag shape. Lay the bent section of wire in the center of the smooth side of the rectangle. Press gently to slightly embed the wire. **3.** Lay the second rectangle on top of the first, textured side up. Press gently to adhere them together. Trim away any uneven edges. Leave this rectangle in place on the index card and set it aside. **4.** Combine a quarter-sized ball of the Off-White clay and add very small pinches of Green and Turquoise clay for a pale Blue-Green color. Roll this piece of clay on a very thin setting. Place it on an index card. Dust it with corn starch. Use the rubber stamp to impress the word into the clay. • Lightly tap the Olive inkpad over the clay to highlight the letters. Bake the stamped clay word on the index card at 275° for 20 minutes. Let it cool. **5.** Brush a little Liquid Clay on the back of the baked word and center it on the Off-White rectangle. Press gently to adhere the pieces. Bake the piece on the index card at 275° for 30 minutes. Let cool.

6. Dust the moon face mold with a little cornstarch. Roll a small ball of the off-White clay. Follow the package instructions on the mold to create the face for your pendant. Use a shader brush to apply a small amount of the Pale Pink chalk to the cheeks and lips. Use a toothpick and some Black chalk to define the pupil of the eyes. Set the face aside. **7.** Roll a sheet of Off-White clay through the pasta machine at a medium setting and trim this sheet to 3" x 4". Repeat this step with a sheet of Black clay. Place the Off-White sheet on top of the Black, smoothing it into place with your fingers to avoid trapping air bubbles. **8.** Cut this rectangle in half and stack again. You should now have a stack with 4 different layers. **9.** Cut the block in half and stack two more times, always stacking Black on top of Off-White. Press gently to adhere the layers together. Use a clay blade to trim away any uneven edges.

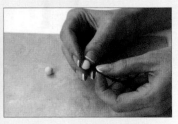

10. Roll a thin sheet of Black clay backing 3" wide. Cut several thin slices from the side of the striped block and place them on the Black sheet. Roll lightly with the acrylic rod to adhere the striped pieces to the Black clay backing. With the stripes running vertically, run this sheet through the pasta machine at progressively thinner settings. When you have a very thin sheet, cut two ³⁄₈" wide strips from the sheet. **11.** Brush a little Liquid Clay along the sides of the baked rectangle and lay the striped clay strips into place. Trim excess. Cut a thin tapered strip from the striped clay sheet and apply it to the moon face, curving it into place. Bake both of the clay pieces on an index card at 275° for 30 minutes. Let cool. **12.** Drill a hole from the top to the bottom of the moon face. Add some coordinating beads to the Silver wire on the body and insert the wire through the bottom of the mold-ed face. Use the pliers to make a loop large enough to accommodate the necklace cord. Wrap the wire around the base of the loop to secure. Form the remaining wire into a spiral shape with pliers. **13.** Roll two ½" balls from the remaining Blue-Green clay. Use the needle tool to pierce the balls, but be careful not to pierce all the way through them. Bake them on a piece of polyester batting at 275° for 30 minutes. String the buna cord through the wire loop in your pendant. Slide the o-ring over both ends of the cord. • Brush a little glue on the ends of the cord and insert them into the baked balls of clay. Adjust the cord by sliding the o-ring up and down.

Butterfly Necklace
Maria Del Pinto

Pendant with Sparkle

Simply gorgeous! Golden butterflies sparkle with the radiance of Austrian crystal.

MATERIALS:
Kato Polymer Clay (3 oz. Gold, 3 oz. Green) • 12 Diamond shaped 4mm crystals • 4 Jet Black 4mm cube beads • Gunmetal seed beads • Delica Gunmetal Purple-Gold hex beads • 12 *Swarovski* Clear 10mm Austrian Crystal flat-back rhinestones • 10 Gold 5mm jump rings • Gold chain • Gold barrel clasp • *Jacquard* Interference Gold Pearl-Ex powdered pigment • 6 Gold 1" eye pins • 20 gauge Gold wire • Deeply etched rubber stamp • 2 styles Butterfly cookie cutters • Pliers (Needle-nose, Round-nose) • Wire cutter • Soft mop brush • Wax paper • Super Glue

Wire Pieces

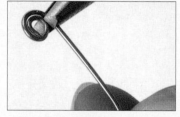 

1. Spirals: Cut 1½" Gold wire. Use round-nose pliers to curl 1 end into a ¹⁄₁₆" circle. **2.** With needle-nose pliers, continue the flat spiral until it is approximately ¼" in diameter. Bend the last ½" of wire at a 90° angle. This will be used to attach spiral to clay. Make 3 more spirals.

3. Wing Wires: Cut two 1⅜" wires for the wings. With round-nose pliers, bend ¼" of the end at 90°. Load the wire with Gunmetal seed beads. Bend the other end. This will be used to attach beads to clay. Repeat to make 2. Set aside spirals and wing wires for use on the Green butterfly. Make 2 wing wires for the Gold butterfly as above, using the Purple-Gold seed beads. Set aside for Gold butterfly. **4. Body Wires**: Cut one 1" length of the wire. Bend a 90° angle at one end. Load the length with a Gunmetal seed bead, crystal, Gunmetal seed bead, crystal, and a Gunmetal seed bead. Bend the other end at a 90° angle. Set aside for Green butterfly. Repeat for Gold butterfly, using Purple-Gold seed beads and crystals. Set aside for Gold butterfly.

Maria Del Pinto

Maria is a free-lance designer, product demonstrator, and teacher. She has made several television appearances on both DIY Network and HGTV. See her travel and workshop schedule at

www.delpinto.com.

5. Connectors: Cut two 1" lengths of wire. Using the round-nose pliers, bend the wire into a circle at the end. Load the length with a crystal, cube bead, and a crystal. **6.** Bend the other end of the wire into a circle. Repeat for a total of 4. Set aside.

Butterfly Pendants

1. Condition all the clay thoroughly before using. Mix colors Metallic Green: (Color Formula for Greenish Butterfly: 2 parts Green and 1 part Gold) and roll on the thickest setting. Cut a 2" x 4" rectangle from each piece and lay on wax paper. Lightly spray the Gold clay surface with <u>automotive protectant fluid</u> and spread it out with your fingers. **2.** Press clay onto the deeply etched rubber stamp. Carefully peel off rectangle and make sure you have a deeply impressed pattern. Repeat with Green clay.

3. Cut each rectangle in half. Place the unstamped sides together to create a double-sided butterfly. **4.** Use the larger cookie cutter to cut out the Gold butterfly. Use the smaller cookie cutter to cut out the Green butterfly. **5.** Carefully brush the surface of the Green butterfly with pigment powder. **6.** Take the Green butterfly wire centerpiece and carefully brush the ends with Super Glue. Attach by pushing the wire into the clay. Repeat for the body wire.

7. Place the flat-back crystals and the decorative wire spiral pieces into the clay in a pleasing pattern. **8.** Repeat for Gold butterfly. Press the Gunmetal seed beads and flat crystals into the clay in a pleasing pattern. Mark the center point of each wing on both butterflies, and insert the eye pin into each wing. Gently place butterflies in the oven and bake at 275° for 90 minutes. Remove from oven. Let cool.

Necklace Assembly

1. Pull out one eye pin and lightly coat it with Super Glue. Insert it back into the butterfly. Repeat for all eye pins. Glue loose spirals and crystals to butterflies and eye pins. **2. Assembly:** Slide the end link of a connector wire onto a jump ring. • Attach each connector wire to the eye pins on the Gold butterfly. Use jump rings to attach the top of the connectors to the Green butterfly. Attach the other 2 connectors to the top of the Green butterfly. Cut two 10" chain segments, each with the same number of links. Use jump rings to attach the necklace chain. Attach clasp with jump rings.

Hot Air
Balloons
Herbal
Bracelets
Clay Figure

Leslie Blackford

MATERIALS:

Kato Translucent Polyclay (Black, White, Orange, Green) • Black buna cord • Burnt Umber oil paint • Needle tool • Skewer • Adhesive

1. Condition clays. Pinch a ball of Black clay into a head shape. **2.** Shape White clay into a beak. Attach beak to head. **3.** Smooth join with fingers.

4. Use a needle tool to draw feather marks onto head. **5.** Roll Green and Terra Cotta clay into logs. Cut 4 Terra Cotta pieces 2¼" long for legs. Cut 2 Green pieces 2" long for arms. Add elbow bend to arms. Pierce a 1" hole into ends of arms and lower leg pieces with needle tool. **6.** Pierce a hole all the way through the upper leg pieces with a skewer. The hole must be large enough for the cord to pass through.

7. Shape Black clay into hands and feet and add to the ends of arm and lower leg pieces. Roll White clay on a thin setting. Cut into ¼" wide strips. Cover joins on hands and feet with strips. **8.** Roll a log of scrap clay for the body.

Patterned cane for shirt: Roll a sheet of each clay on a medium setting. Layer clays on a ceramic tile. Brayer between layers to remove bubbles. Cut sheet in half and stack. Slice edges to straighten. Roll into a ½" log. Pinch into triangle shape. Cut thin slices and apply to front of body log.

Jacket: Roll Green clay on medium setting. Wrap clay around body. Shape to create coat. Attach head to body. Make collar line with needle tool. Shape jacket tails so bird can sit up. Add small balls of Terra cotta for buttons. Make buttonholes with needle tool. Pierce a hole large enough for cord to pass all the way through the upper body for arm cord. Pierce two 1" holes into lower body for leg cords. Bake at 275° for 30 minutes. Rub all pieces with Burnt Umber to age. Wipe with a soft cloth.

9. Adhere cord into one lower leg piece. Pass through an upper leg piece, trim and glue end into lower body hole. Repeat for other leg. Pass cord through upper body. Glue 1 arm to end of cord. Trim. Glue other arm in place.

Clay Figure

by Leslie Blackford

Definitely distinctive, this figure sports a stylish patterned shirt and fancy topcoat. Figures are simple to make using clay tubes and buna cord.

Herbal Clay Bracelets

by Leslie Blackford

Fun to wear chunky beads in citrus colors form bracelets with sweet natural scents.

MATERIALS: Kato Translucent Polyclay • *Ranger* Adirondack alcohol inks (Meadow, Denim, Wild Plum, Butterscotch, Pesto, Red Pepper, Current, Mushroom, Cranberry, Caramel, Lettuce) • Essential Oils (Peppermint, Lavender, Chamomile, Thyme, Rose, Lemon) • Dried herbs (mint, thyme, lavender, chamomile, finely crushed rose petals) • Black buna cord • Oil base paint (Raw Umber, Burnt Sienna) • Needle tool • Toothpick • Cotton swab • Old toothbrush • Soft cloth

How to Prepare Clay

1. Condition clay. Roll on thick setting. Drip inks onto clay. **2.** Spread inks with cotton swab. Let dry. **3.** Fold clay with the inks on the inside. **4.** Roll on thick setting. Continue folding and rolling until the clay is a uniform color.

5. Sprinkle herbs and essential oils onto clay. Let stand for a few minutes to allow oil to soak into herbs. **6.** Fold one side over. **7.** Fold other side over to form a pocket for herbs. Roll on thick setting. **8.** Continue to fold and roll until herbs are evenly distributed.

Leslie Blackford

Leslie's unique, primitive style distinguishes her sculptural polymer clay art. Recently published in 3 books, she travels across the country teaching workshops.

How to Make a Scarab Bead

1. Prepare the clay. Roll it into a log. **2.** Cut the log into sections. **3.** Roll each section into a ball. **4.** Shape each ball into a flattened oval.

5. SCARAB PATTERN: Use a toothpick to mark a line in back two-thirds of shape. **6.** Mark across scarab just above the back mark. **7.** Make a second line above the first. **8.** Pick up scarab and mark around the edges.

9. Make several more lines on the face portion. **10.** Use a needle tool or pointed toothpick to make a hole halfway through the piece, from the head to the tail. Remove tool and make other half of hole from the other end. Bake at 275° for 30 minutes. Let cool. **11.** Mix 1 part Raw Umber paint with 1 part Burnt Sienna. Work into clay with an old toothbrush. **12.** Wipe with a soft cloth.

Herbal Formulas

Mint Clay
1 oz. Translucent clay
15 -20 drops Meadow ink
1 teaspoon dried mint leaves
5-10 drops peppermint essential oil

Chamomile Clay
1 oz. Translucent clay
15 drops Butterscotch ink
1 teaspoon dried chamomile
4-5 drops chamomile essential oil

Rose Clay
1 oz. Translucent clay
3 drops each Red Pepper, Currant, Mushroom, Cranberry ink
1 teaspoon rose petals
5-6 drops rose essential oil

Lavender Clay
1 oz. Translucent clay
10-15 drops Denim ink
4-5 drops Wild Plum ink
1 teaspoon dried lavender buds
5-6 drops lavender essential oil

Thyme Clay
1 oz Translucent clay
15 drops Pesto ink
½-1 oz. dried thyme leaves
2-3 drops thyme essential oil (Thyme oil is extremely potent, use caution.)

Citrus Clay
1 oz. Translucent clay
4 drops each Caramel and Butterscotch ink
2 drops Lettuce ink
10 drops lemon or orange essential oil

MATERIALS:
Kato (Liquid Clay; Polyclay: 2 oz. Red, 2 oz. Metallic Gold, 1 oz. White, OR 2 oz. Green, 2 oz. Magenta, 2 oz. White) • Cord • 3" Vanity light bulb • Raw Umber oil paint • Tracing wheel • Screwdriver • Tack hammer • Freezer bag • *Kemper* cutters (⅞" circle, star) • Drill • 1/16" drill bit

ADDITIONAL MATERIALS:
Small 3" figure to hang from the balloon. Make one from clay or use a small purchased figure.

INSTRUCTIONS:
Condition clay. Roll Red clay on thickest setting. Cover light bulb, excluding metal stem, with clay. Trim excess and smooth. • Roll out White clay on medium setting. Cut out stars and place on top half of the balloon. • Cut 6 small rectangles of White clay. Place evenly around the base of the balloon.

Roll out Metallic Gold clay on thin setting. Cut ½" strips with tracing wheel. Wrap around the balloon at the top and bottom of the rectangles. Texture with needle tool.

Roll a ½" ball of Metallic Gold. Shape into a square and adhere to the top of the balloon with Liquid Polyclay. Pierce center of square with needle tool to fit cord. Make another hole in the opposite side, just above, for the hanger. Pierce a small hole in each side of the base.

Make 3 small logs, 1 Red, 1 Gold, 1 White. Twist together and roll into a thin cord. Wrap the cord around the base of the square and above the bottom strip of Gold. • Bake at 285° for 30 minutes. Let cool completely in oven.

Place balloon in a freezer bag. Place the end of the screwdriver between the edge of the clay and the metal on the bulb. Tap screwdriver with hammer until metal breaks off. Gently tap the balloon, breaking the interior glass. Remove from bag and rinse to remove all glass shards. • Redrill holes as needed.

Antique with Raw Umber. • Thread cord through top of balloon, down the sides and through the holes in the bottom. Attach cords to figure. • String hanger through upper holes in the top of the balloon.

Hot Air Balloons

by Leslie Blackford

Cheerful figures dangle from colorful hot air balloons. Create a collection of colorful balloons, you'll love seeing them hang in every room of your home, or give one as a unique gift.

1. Cover a vanity light bulb with clay. Do Not cover the metal stem. **2.** Cut off the excess clay. **3.** Smooth the surface until it is uniform. **4.** Create wedges and texture with a tracing wheel and a needle tool. **5.** After balloon is baked, place the balloon in a freezer bag. Use a screwdriver and hammer to break the metal part off the bulb. Remove from the bag

*Zippered Vase
Spoon Pendants
Treasure Box*

Sue Kelsey

Sue Kelsey

Sue is a working artist and designer with 22 years of experience in production work for juried craft shows and galleries. She is a product demonstrator at HIA and CHA. See her work at

www.suekelsey.com

Metallic Vase with a Working Zipper

by Sue Kelsey

Intrigue guests with an eclectic sculptural vase. The dimension and texture attract the hand before the eye even finishes examining the flowing lines in this interesting work of art. The zipper really opens! The molded leaves at the top and base are fabulous to feel and lovely to behold.

MATERIALS:

Kato (Repel Gel; Liquid Polyclay; Polyclay: 6 oz Black, 3 oz. Gold, 3 oz. Silver, 3 oz. Copper, 2 oz Light color for zipper pattern) • *Walnut Hollow* Makins' (Leaf push mold; Professional Clay tool set: small sphere, rounded point) • 10"-12" tall straight sided vase • 18"- 20" heavy weight metal zipper • Size 24 stainless steel straight pins • *Loew Cornell* brushes (½" wash, ¾" mop) • Corn starch

1. Condition the scrap clay and roll on a medium setting on your pasta machine. Press the zipper on the clay to imprint the zipper teeth. Cut around the zipper for pattern. **2.** Spiral wrap the pattern around the vase leaving a 2" overhang on the top. Trim the bottom if zipper pattern is too long. Press to secure pattern to the vase. Bake according to manufacturer's instructions for 30 minutes. Let cool. **3.** Apply a thin coat of Repel Gel over the top of the zipper pattern. Let dry. **4.** Make a Skinner Blend of Black, Gold, Copper, and Silver. See page 3. **5.** Roll out on medium setting.

 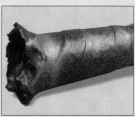   

6. Trim blend into a rectangle. **7.** Wrap the clay around the vase covering the zipper pattern, leaving about 2 inches over the top and bottom of the vase. **8.** Fold clay over the bottom of vase. Remove the excess bulk, with a clay blade, making sure that the bottom of vase is smooth. **9.** Smooth out the bottom of vase until it stands flat. **10.** With a clay blade, remove a ⅝" strip of the clay down the middle of the zipper template.

11. Stipple the raw clay with a small sphere and a round pointed tool (the end of a paintbrush works great). Bake at 275° for 1 hour. **12.** When the vase is still slightly warm, remove the clay from the vase. Carefully remove the zipper pattern and place the clay back on the vase to cool completely. Make sure the zipper is closed. **13.** Carefully position the cloth zipper where the clay pattern was removed. Secure with straight pins. If needed, trim the zipper at the bottom. **14.** Apply a small amount of Liquid Polyclay to the lower part of the zipper just under the clay rim. Do this all the way down the zipper.
Bake the clay covered vase at 275° for 1 hour. Let cool.
Turn the vase over and do the same thing to the upper side of the zipper.
Bake upside down for 1 hour. This will keep the Liquid Polyclay from oozing into the zipper teeth making it impossible to open. Let cool.

15. Dust the leaf mold with cornstarch. Press leftover clay into the mold. Indent the veins with a shaping tool. Remove leaf from the mold. Shape leaf to fit the vase. **16.** Remove leaf and apply Liquid Polyclay to the leaf where it will touch the vase. **17.** Adhere leaves to the top of the vase with Liquid Polyclay. **18.** Adhere leaves to the bottom of the vase with Liquid Polyclay. **19.** Adhere additional leaves with Liquid Polyclay if desired.
Bake at 275° for 1 hour.

Treasure Box

by Sue Kelsey

Why would you want an ordinary trinket box when you can have an extraordinary work of art on your table or dresser? Make a Treasure Box to hold precious keepsakes or give this one as a gift.

MATERIALS:
Kato Polyclay (Silver, Pearl, Gold, Green, Turquoise, Purple) • *Craft Supply USA* 2½" round box hinge • Tin box 2¼" tall x 2½" diameter • *Walnut Hollow* Makins' Dot Texture sheet • *Polymer Clay Express* Round cutters (2½", 2¾") • *Kemper* Small round cutter • *Loew Cornell* (Synthetic steel wool; Brushes: ½" wash, ¾" mop) • Corn starch • *Liquid Nails* 5 minute epoxy • *Crafters Pick* The Ultimate! glue

1. Condition Silver clay and roll two coils ¼" x 9" long. **2.** Place the coils in the recess of the hinge. Trim and smooth clay. This will be the grout that holds the tin in place. **3.** Place the tin box top into the clay and gently push down to secure. Repeat with the bottom tin. **4.** Turn over the hinged box and check the inside to be sure the Silver clay didn't ooze into the inside. Gently remove excess clay. Bake at 275° for 30 minutes. Let cool. Brush the entire box with The Ultimate! glue. Let dry.

5. Mix your background clay and roll on the thickest setting. **6.** Cut out one strip 1" x 8½" for the sides of the bottom, one strip ½" x 8½" for the sides of the top, one 2½" bottom circle, and one 2¾" top circle. **7.** Cover the bottom with the small circle. Smooth out air bubbles. Wrap the bottom side strip around the tin and smooth seams. **8.** Repeat for top.

Clay Recipes:

Background:
Condition 4 oz. Pearl, ¼ oz. Green and a pinch of Turquoise. Mix together to a uniform color.

Leaves or Reeds:
Condition ½ oz. Gold and ½ oz. Green. Mix together to a uniform color.

Flowers:
Condition ¼ oz. Purple and ½ oz. Pearl, and make a tiny Skinner blend. See page 3.

Keep treasures and trinkets,
jewelry and earrings in
these handy little boxes.

9. Condition and roll out leaf colored clay on a medium setting. Cut out leaves. **10.** Place leaves on the box in a pleasing manner. Gently smooth them into the top and sides of box. Roll out the flower blend on a medium setting. Cut out tiny circles. Position circles on top and bottom of box. **11.** Smooth with roller. **12.** Using synthetic steel wool, texture the whole box, being careful not to distort flowers and leaves.

  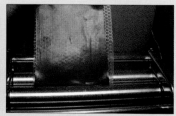 

13. Condition Gold clay. Roll through on incrementally smaller settings to a thin sheet. Clay will be very fragile. Set clay aside to firm up slightly. **14.** Dust the dot texture sheet with corn starch. Tap off excess. Place clay on sheet. **15.** To make clay netting, carefully run a texture sheet and clay through the pasta machine at the same setting as you put your clay through. Go slowly. This will make a bit of a mess, but the pieces are well worth it. **16.** Cut pieces of netting. Place on the box and gently secure with acrylic roller, or synthetic steel wool. If you do this gently, you will still have texture from the netting. Bake the box at 275° for 1 hour. When trinket box is cool, check to be sure that it is secure to the hinges. If the tin is loose, affix the tin to the hinges with 5 minute epoxy.

Spoon Pendants

by Sue Kelsey

From funny to theatrical, sunny to scary, make an array of faces by molding clay on a spoon! Use these fun creations as pendants, pins, or embellishments on cards and gifts.

MATERIALS:
Kato (Liquid Polyclay; Repel Gel; Polyclay: Black, White, Silver, Pearl, Copper; NuBlade) • Buna cord or ball chain • Pin back • *Ranger* Perfect Pearls powder • *Clearsnap* (ColorBox Cool Doodle Stylus; Molding Mat) • *Wilton* 2½" oval cutter • *Kemper* (Pro tool; Ball stylus; Cutters: heart, circle, star) • *Loew Cornell* brushes (wash, mop) • Fine sanding sponge • *Stick Fast* Cyanoacrylate glue

1. With wash brush cover metal spoon with Repel Gel. Let dry. Roll a ³⁄₁₆" ball of clay. Shape into a cone and place on the back of a spoon for a nose. Bake at 275° for 10 minutes.

2. Roll out White clay on medium thin setting. Cut oval with cutter.